TWO AMERICAN PAINTERS

FRITZ SCHOLDER
AND T. C. CANNON

ADELYN D. BREESKIN, CURATOR OF CONTEMPORARY PAINTING AND SCULPTURE

Published for the National Collection of Fine Arts by the Smithsonian Institution Press

City of Washington, 1972

EXHIBITION APRIL 7 —MAY 29, 1972

NATIONAL COLLECTION OF FINE ARTS

SMITHSONIAN INSTITUTION

Library of Congress Catalog Card Number 76–39584

For sale by the Superintendent of Documents,
United States Government Printing Office,
Washington, D.C. 20402—Price $1.25   Stock number   4703-0013

COVER: Fritz Scholder, *Buffalo Dancer*. catalog number 16   FRONTISPIECE: Fritz Scholder, *Indians #19*. catalog number 3

CONTENTS

FOREWORD

To refer to Fritz Scholder and T. C. Cannon as "Indian artists" is to obscure a more significant point. They belong very much to the contemporary world of art and embrace the full range of consciousness of which it is aware. While their medium is often the Indian, their subject ultimately is man everywhere. In general, they belong to that kind of painting which came to the fore in the decade of the sixties to stand against the concept that art was a matter of reassuring perfection and aesthetic contemplation, in favor of an art that prodded both the outer and inner environments of contemporary urban life. There is an awareness of "Pop," the force of vulgarity, of the haunting environmental textures of Jasper Johns and Rauschenberg, and of the crushing terror of Bacon and the more personal loneliness of Diebenkorn, Oliveira, and the San Francisco painters. But that is only the setting; as painters neither Scholder nor Cannon fall readily into a school.

Scholder and Cannon may well have had to face up to two temptations in the paths they have chosen in their recent paintings. One, which has doomed so many socially conscious artists, is the tendency to deal with man in society in grossly simple schematic terms, blunting the very human consciousness they seek to preserve. The other is the temptation to establish self-consciously an "Indian" art, to sacrifice their personal awareness in order to formulate an ethnic cliché. If these were, indeed, temptations they have been avoided by these two painters. Although the social group may be the context and may even have provoked the individual problems in a very specific sense, it is the individual human state that comes through, and we make it our own.

Scholder's painting followed a consistent path, moving from a discovery of the coincidence between his painterly world and the landscape around him to a more telling coincidence with the interior landscape of human feeling. His rich sense of pattern and surprising interplay of color become a subtle means of evocation, often provoking a sense of precariousness that causes both the eye and the mind to ponder rather than to judge. In some of his most memorable works he plays with a stock image of the Indian, not to ridicule it or discard it—it is a fact of mind, also for Indians—but to get beneath it. There is nothing funnier, or more poignant, than a public symbol caught up in the malaise of existence. Humor is one of Scholder's most appealing qualities, but it is not satire in any simple manner of speaking. While he may despise pretense, he does not hate the pretender nor even suggest that he wishes to reform him. And much of his humor springs from the surprise of incongruity which, like any good story, cannot quite be explained away. It is an integral part of the earthly vitality that pervades his work, which is sometimes violent to the point of self-destruction, sometimes lyrical, and occasionally penetratingly comic.

There is something rather more stern in the works of T. C. Cannon. His paintings exist in a tension that arrests the action in an emphatic and unrelenting image. At first glance, there is a matter-of-factness that would seem to preclude imagining or introspection, but the harsh statement provokes its own kind of unsentimental compassion and strange poetry. Although he began his serious painting under Scholder, Cannon presents a different world—a world into which one is not sensuously drawn, but in which the mind is confronted with stark visions that compel attention and demand a personal commitment.

Drawing upon the particularities of their backgrounds yet speaking in the idiom common to their time, these two artists have made a distinct contribution to American art.

JOSHUA C. TAYLOR
Director
National Collection of Fine Arts

ACKNOWLEDGMENTS

Since the world of today is attuned to youth, it seems appropriate that we feature in this exhibition paintings by two young artists. One of them, T.C. Cannon, is twenty-five years of age. His art career is just beginning after more than six years of special study and a tour of duty in Vietnam with the 101st Air Cavalry. The other of our two artists, Fritz Scholder, nine years older than Cannon, has already gained an enviable place as the acknowledged leader of the New Indian Painting Group. When asked with whom he would like to share an exhibition, without hesitation he chose his former pupil, T. C. Cannon.

Robert A. Ewing as Curator-in-charge of Fine Arts at the Museum of New Mexico in Santa Fe has known both artists well and has followed their progress during the past seven years. We are most grateful to him for his interesting introductory essay.

We thank the Institute of American Indian Arts, Santa Fe, New Mexico, and the Southern Plains Indian Museum and Crafts Center, Anadarko, Oklahoma, for their help with photographs and data. The Bureau of Indian Affairs and the Indian Arts and Crafts Board of the United States Department of the Interior, Washington, D.C., were also helpful in supplying us with information.

We thank Mr. Joachim Jean Aberbach, a most enthusiastic patron of Fritz Scholder's work, and Mr. Arne H. Ekstrom of Cordier & Ekstrom, Inc., for their generous help toward increasing the number of illustrations in the catalog.

To all of the lenders, we owe our warmest thanks. We are fully aware that depriving them of their paintings for an extensive period of time demanded a sacrifice on their part.

Other acknowledgments include thanks to the two artists whose collaboration has been of much help to us, to Jan K. Muhlert and Florine E. Lyons for their help with catalog preparation, to Georgia Rhoades for editorial assistance, and to Harry Lowe for his gifted installation.

ADELYN D. BREESKIN
Curator of Contemporary Painting and Sculpture
National Collection of Fine Arts

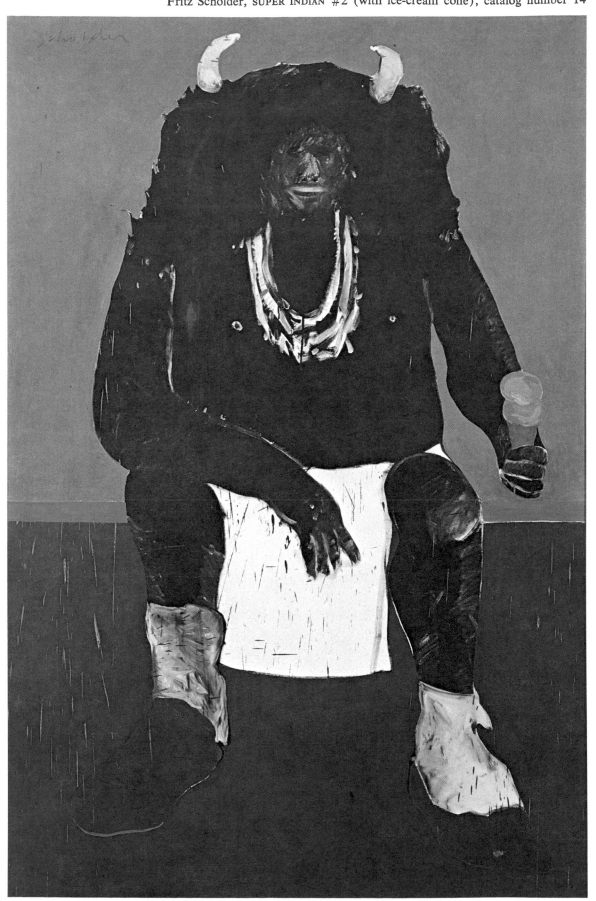

NEW INDIAN ART

I believe . . . that there is a new Indian art emerging. It will take many forms and will be vital. A merging of traditional subject matter with the contemporary idioms will give us a truer statement of the Indian.[1]

FRITZ SCHOLDER

The American Indian embodies the soul of this continent, and is one of the most compelling and disturbing elements of the conglomerate American culture. Ruthlessly exploited and almost destroyed by the European invaders, the Indian has survived as a symbol of that which is good in men who live in contact with the earth. As a quasi-mystical source of inspiration in the arts, the Indian is "in" in the 1960s and 1970s in the United States of America.

The art of the American Indian closely parallels his varied and turbulent history. The first art objects of the Indian were created as part of an unselfconscious everyday life. Clothing, habitations, and ceremonial objects were made from the materials at hand such as fur, feathers, shell, and clay. Taken out of their natural environments, these objects are proudly displayed in museums as a distinguished part of man's total art production.

The disruption forced by the confrontation of European civilization with the inhabitants of the "New World" effectively destroyed the Indian way of life as it had been. The simpler culture invaded by a complex civilization was presented with so much which was new that a large part of the Indian world succumbed before it could adapt to inevitable changes. Alcohol and smallpox aptly symbolize the negative aspects of the new influences, but there were positive qualities to the changing Indian world. For example, the introduction of silver and wool to the Navajo people made possible one of the most beautiful periods of Indian art production.

Historically, the Indian as a painter provided decoration for ceremonial structures such as the kivas of the Southwest, decorated habitations such as the Plains Indian tepee, and left his messages in picture writing or in the pictographs and petroglyphs which still mark the sheltered rock walls of our country. In the early part of this century, Indian painting, encouraged by non-Indian artists and ethnologists, became an important part of the American art scene. In the valley of the Rio Grande, where the Pueblo Indians had managed to preserve a great deal of their ceremonial life and where two major art colonies—Taos and Santa Fe—were located, this "traditional" Indian painting became one of the happy moments in the post-conquest history of the American Indian.

[1] C.R. Wenzell, *Artists of Santa Fe,* 1969, p. 42.

FRITZ SCHOLDER

T.C. CANNON

12

Painted on paper with opaque watercolor, the traditional Indian painting of the first part of this century is a vivid and beautiful record of everyday and ceremonial life. Indian painters had an extraordinary sense of design and their work was the obvious continuation of the art heritage of their people.

Unfortunately, well-meaning teachers directed young Indians into what had become an "official" style, and the life went out of this very special period of Indian art. By the 1940s "traditional" Indian painting had become self-consciously charming and childlike, and a patronizing attitude on the part of collectors encouraged the repetition of a cliché vocabulary of symbols and subjects.

In the cultural chaos of the years following World War II, a few young Indian artists began working with the materials and ideas of contemporary art. The war had taken them physically into the larger world, and the acceleration of communications brought that world into every Indian home.

In the early 1960s, a group of gifted young Indian creators were brought together in the important Rockfeller Project which was held at the University of Arizona at Tucson. The project was an experimental probe of the thesis that Indian traditions could be combined with contemporary idioms and techniques, and it provided the impetus for the establishment of the Institute of American Indian Arts in Santa Fe by the Bureau of Indian Affairs in 1962.

Fritz Scholder was an enthusiastic participant in the Rockefeller Project who later became an instructor at the Institute. Scholder had gained a reputation as an exciting contemporary painter and was determined to be known not as an *Indian* painter but as an uncategorized artist. IIis list of accomplishments and awards qualified him as a painting teacher and his Mission-Indian heritage gave him the requisite rapport with his students. Scholder painted series, and he came to Santa Fe in the midst of his "stripe" period. His canvases then were completely abstract and consisted of layers of soft-edged stripes which evoked the stratification of the land. The colors were vibrant, the technique innovative. Splatters of color, or of turpentine, softened the divisions and produced glowing passages of pure paint.

The world which Scholder entered at the Institute was saturated with things Indian. The credo of the school was, and is, to provide the young Indian with a thorough knowledge of his people's heritage while training him to live in and use the materials of his time. Classes in traditional Indian dance alternated with modern dance. At one memorable performance, a young actor was painted half red and half white and then almost literally pulled apart by traditional drums on one side of the stage and blaring transistor radios on the other.

Classes in design transposed motifs from old pots and baskets to produce yards of boldly abstract textiles. Jewelry students used traditional silver and turquoise to produce innovative contemporary necklaces and bracelets. A design student stepped into various colors of paint and created a mono-print by dancing on long strips of paper. Before anyone had coined the phrase "Red Power" there was a pride in being young and Indian, and the students and faculty were filled with vitality and dreams.

In spite of his declared separation from Indian themes, Scholder began collecting Indian arti-facts and attending the extraordinary dances in the nearby pueblos. His classes in the history of art were attracting a group of young followers, and as a painting teacher he knew when to encour-age his students and when to let them alone. He changed his subject matter to *butterflies*—huge butterflies glowing with color and covered with intertwining rivulets and spatters of color. The butterflies were his last holdout against the inevitable subject of the American Indian.

The students at the Institute, although part of an ethnic group, emerged as individuals with separate abilities and personal dreams. One of the most exciting was a seventeen-year-old Caddo/Kiowa from Oklahoma then called Tommy Cannon, later T. C. Cannon. Tommy had grown up, as a boy might have a hundred years before, with a gun and a pack of dogs and unending river bottoms to explore. The "Media," as he terms it—magazines, newspapers, television, the FM sta-tion late at night—opened his town of three hundred to a much bigger world. He had always read, and from the age of ten he drew steadily. He knew that he would work in the arts, but the Institute provided his first real art teachers.

T. C. was one of Scholder's most avid students and remembers him as a magnificent art-history teacher. One of T. C.'s student paintings places an abstracted but recognizable Scholder against a background of brilliant stripes. The advanced painting students were assigned small studios which they decorated to fit their enthusiasms, and Cannon worked in an area which he purged of all but the really inquisitive by playing Bob Dylan records at full volume. He was a great fan of the Bay Area painters, and his painting heroes were the giants of the time—Diebenkorn, Parks, Rivers, Johns, and Rauschenberg. He was looking for his own world, and in Scholder he had a sympathetic and enthusiastic teacher to help him in his search. His turning point was a painting called *Mama and Papa Have the Going Home to Shiprock Blues* (cat. no. 29). A large painting of an Indian couple waiting for a bus, it could only be called "Indian Pop Art."

After the butterflies, Scholder finally began to use Indian subjects in his paintings. The first Indians were small and somehow tentative. He was looking for his own approach to subjects which had become clichés. As he began to find his way his paintings grew larger and a definite style emerged. His brush strokes became increasingly simplified, as his subject matter became more complex. In one huge painting, an Indian is juxtaposed with the completely unexpected, a rhi-noceros, and boldly scrawled "BIA" (cat. no. 4). "Insane" Indians and "Monster" Indians shocked

14

the traditionalists and delighted the iconoclasts. Scholder and his students exchanged ideas and enthusiasms, and there was the wonderful mutual discovery that they had found a way to express their feelings about being Indian in the United States of America in the 1960s.

After graduation Cannon went to San Francisco to continue his studies and entered what he now calls the worst period in his life. After the freshness and vitality of the Institute, he had expected enlightened minds and found "a lot of people doing nothing but talking." The Indian group in San Francisco had a well-defined region in the city with their own bars and "pow wows on Market Street," and he found himself losing the impetus he had found in Santa Fe. His dilemma was resolved when he was drafted and after training at Fort Lewis, Washington, where the scenery kept him alive, he was sent to Vietnam. In Vietnam he kept notebooks of poems and sketches, and often in a thumbnail sketch would try to remember a particular painting from his art-history classes: Marat assassinated in his tub or Gauguin's yellow Christ mixed with his own dreams and ideas for paintings.

In the late sixties Scholder also left the Institute, initially to make his first trip to Europe and then to begin work as a full-time painter. The commitment and power in his painting made him the acknowledged leader in the New Indian Art movement, and success followed·success. He has been written about extensively, and his personal philosophy has matured as he has produced a succession of brilliant paintings. He wraps Indians in American flags and paints them in the desolate bars of Gallup, New Mexico. The figures are often grotesque, and comic-strip balloons bear such "in" joke messages as "Dog Stew, Yum, Yum!" Scholder feeds on controversy and notoriety. He has developed a life style to match his painting and obviously delights in shocking people, but always with the intent of making them think. Besieged by collectors, museums, and plain curiosity seekers, he has played the part of the celebrity with an air of casual self-assurance. The important thing in his life is his work, and his paintings consistently surprise and delight his following.

T. C. Cannon returned to New Mexico after being discharged from the Armed Forces and with a minimum of adjustment began producing his own "New Indian" art. His first one-man exhibition in Santa Fe revealed his personal painting viewpoint. His first paintings after leaving the service carried more of the sadness of the history of the Indian than did those of his peers. A severed head with the mouth filled with grass is a painting of Andrew Myrick, an Indian agent who, when told that the people were starving, said, "Let them eat grass" (cat. no. 30). In another painting called *Soldiers* (cat. no. 32), half of a figure is an Indian warrior and the other half a soldier in blue. Poignant and deeply moving, the paintings carry great promise for Cannon's future. A creative man in many senses of the word, Cannon keeps notebooks of poems and the sketches which grow into his major paintings. His poems are extremely personal and are indicative of the very special man he is.

In 1967, T. C. Cannon wrote a poem dedicated to his teacher:

(upon viewing all of the numbers that are new mexico's face)
(for fritz)

sprinkles of silver beads
on turquoise mountains
have collected in the crevice of your eye
pushing out from you
the land stripe
and banners
with sipapu written through their faces

if such had but a voice
it would sing,
    "it's here, it's here."

In 1968, he wrote:

art . . . being the fiend that it is
wraps me in a bundle
and sends me off
to the house of myself.

Born of a lyric heritage and feeding on the passions of our revolutionary times, the New Indian Art promises to become an important movement in American art. The Indian is a stirring subject, and books such as *Custer Died for Your Sins, Bury My Heart at Wounded Knee,* and *Little Big Man,* attempt to right the wrongs of our past history. The paintings of Fritz Scholder and T. C. Cannon thrust the viewer into a confrontation with the bold and provocative art forms of today's Indian artist. Scholder is the leader of the movement and Cannon his most important student. Quoted recently in the *South Dakota Review* published by the University of South Dakota (1971), Scholder said "The work sometimes has a monstrous quality to it, for there is still much torment in the minds of the New Indians. It is sometimes serene, for the Indian person is naturally reticent . . . . If one had to use a single word to describe the Indian today, it would be PARADOX!"

ROBERT A. EWING
Curator-in-charge of Fine Arts
Museum of New Mexico

BIOGRAPHICAL NOTES

FRITZ SCHOLDER

Fritz Scholder was born on October 6, 1937, in Breckenridge, Minnesota, the son of Fritz William Scholder IV who was of German, California Mission Indian (Luiseño), and French descent. His father was an administrator of the local Indian school and had his career in the Bureau of Indian Affairs.

From early childhood, Fritz identified as an artist and won his first prize for a Veterans' Day poster while in the fourth grade. When the family moved to Peoria, South Dakota, he studied with Oscar Howe, the well-known Sioux artist, who introduced him to modern painting. Later, during 1957–1958, he studied with Wayne Thiebaud at Sacramento State College, and while there had his first one-man show at the college art gallery and sold his first painting. In 1960 he received his Bachelor of Arts degree and two years later moved to Tucson to work at the University of Arizona, teaching design and drawing as a graduate assistant while he obtained his Master of Fine Arts degree. Meanwhile, he entered many exhibitions and won a full scholarship to participate in the Southwest Indian Art Project under the auspices of the Rockefeller Foundation. During its second summer session he became a faculty member.

In 1962 he received a John Hay Whitney Opportunity Fellowship and about this time his work drew the attention of James Johnson Sweeney who gave him a Ford Foundation Purchase Award at the Houston Museum ("The Southwest Paintings and Sculpture" competition). Later, Sweeney awarded him first prize at the "West Virginia Centennial Painting Exhibition" in 1963. The following year, Scholder started teaching advanced painting and art history at the Institute of American Indian Arts in Santa Fe, New Mexico. His first paintings of Indians were done in 1967. Meanwhile, he received many more prizes, started exhibiting in New York, and also was included as one of "Three from Santa Fe" at the Center for Arts of Indian America sponsored by the United States Department of the Interior in Washington, D.C.

In 1969, having resigned from the Institute of American Indian Arts in Santa Fe, he and his wife Romona toured through Europe and North Africa for three months. He then saw Francis Bacon's paintings at the Tate Gallery in London, which impressed him deeply. Upon his return, he started devoting all of his time to painting as well as producing much work in lithography after having been invited by the Tamarind Institute to work at its place in Albuquerque. He now has many outlets for his work including the Cordier-Ekstrom Gallery in New York, Esther Bear Gallery in Santa Barbara, The Jamison Galleries in Santa Fe, The Gallery of Contemporary Art in Taos, and the Fendrick Gallery in Washington, D.C. He has won over a dozen awards and has exhibited in over two dozen cities, including four in Europe and two in South America.

17

BIOGRAPHICAL NOTES

T. C. CANNON

T. C. Cannon was born on September 27, 1946, in Lawton, Oklahoma. He attended public schools in Gracemont, Oklahoma, from 1955 to 1964. He then had two years at the Institute of American Indian Arts in Santa Fe. While there he worked with Fritz Scholder and learned much from him. After one year at the San Francisco Art Institute he returned to Santa Fe to attend college there, studying painting and philosophy during 1969–1970, and is now enrolled at Central State University in Edmond, Oklahoma.

Cannon's Indian name is Pai-doung-u-day which means "One Who Stands In the Sun." He developed his interest in art as a child, and remained very close to his traditional Indian heritage. His love of poetry and his creative use of it as a means of expression also stem from his childhood education as a Caddo/Kiowa Indian. Other strong influences in his artistic approach include his art training at the Institute of American Indian Arts and his service with the 101st Air Cavalry in Vietnam for which he was awarded the Bronze Star. His social commentary, now strongly reflected in his work, has been combined with his traditional philosophy.

CATALOG OF THE EXHIBITION

DIMENSIONS ARE IN INCHES AND PARENTHETICALLY IN CENTIMETERS; HEIGHT PRECEDES WIDTH

FRITZ SCHOLDER

PAINTINGS

1 FOUR INDIAN RIDERS 1967
Oil on canvas
60 x 72 (152.4 x 182.9)
Lent by Mr. and Mrs. William H. Metcalf,
Jr., McLean, Virginia
Illustrated on page 23

2 INDIAN #16 1967
Oil on canvas
71 x 71 (180.3 x 180.3)
Lent by Mr. and Mrs. Robert E. Herzstein,
Washington, D.C.
Illustrated on page 24

3 INDIANS #19 1967
Oil on canvas
72 x 61 (182.9 x 154.9)
Collection Eugene B. Adkins, Tulsa, Okla-
homa
Frontispiece illustration in color

4 INDIAN AND RHINOCEROS 1968
Oil on canvas
68 x 120 (172.7 x 304.8)
Lent by Mr. and Mrs. Winthrop Faulkner,
Washington, D.C.

5 SUPER INDIAN 1968
Oil on canvas
120 x 68 (304.8 x 172.7)
Lent by Museum of New Mexico, Santa Fe,
New Mexico
Illustrated on page 25

6 SUPER PUEBLO 1968
Oil on canvas

70 x 80 (177.8 x 203.2)
Lent by Bureau of Indian Affairs, United
States Department of the Interior, Washing-
ton, D.C.

7 INDIAN WITH BEER CAN 1969
Oil on canvas
24 x 24 (60.9 x 60.9)
Lent by Mr. and Mrs. Donald M. Campbell,
Santa Fe, New Mexico
Illustrated on page 26

8 SUPER CHIEF 1969
Oil on canvas
41 x 50 (104.1 x 127.0)
Lent by Mr. and Mrs. Gordon L. Clark,
Mountain View, California

9 AMERICAN INDIAN 1970
Oil on linen
60 x 42 (152.4 x 106.7)
Lent by Indian Arts and Crafts Board, United
States Department of the Interior, Washing-
ton, D.C.

10 INDIAN IN GALLUP 1970
Oil on linen
60 x 54 (152.4 x 137.2)
Lent by Mrs. Marietta Scurry Ransone,
Dallas, Texas

11 INDIANS IN TRANSITION 1970
Oil on canvas
42 x 60 (106.7 x 152.4)
Lent by Dr. and Mrs. Richard B. Streeper,
Santa Fe, New Mexico

12 DOG AND DEAD WARRIOR 1971
    Oil on canvas
    72 x 56   (182.9 x 142.2)
    Lent by the artist

13 INDIAN FOREVER 1971
    Oil on canvas
    70 x 64   (177.8 x 162.6)
    Lent by Mr. and Mrs. Anthony Atwell,
    Dallas, Texas

14 SUPER INDIAN #2
    (with ice-cream cone)   1971
    Oil on canvas
    90 x 60   (228.6 x 152.4)
    Lent by Susan T. and Joachim Jean Aber-
    bach, Sand's Point, Long Island
    Illustrated in color on page 10

15 WOMAN AND CAT 1971
    Oil on canvas
    72 x 56   (182.9 x 142.2)
    Lent by John E. Furen, Houston, Texas
    Illustrated on page 27

15 WOMAN AND CAT

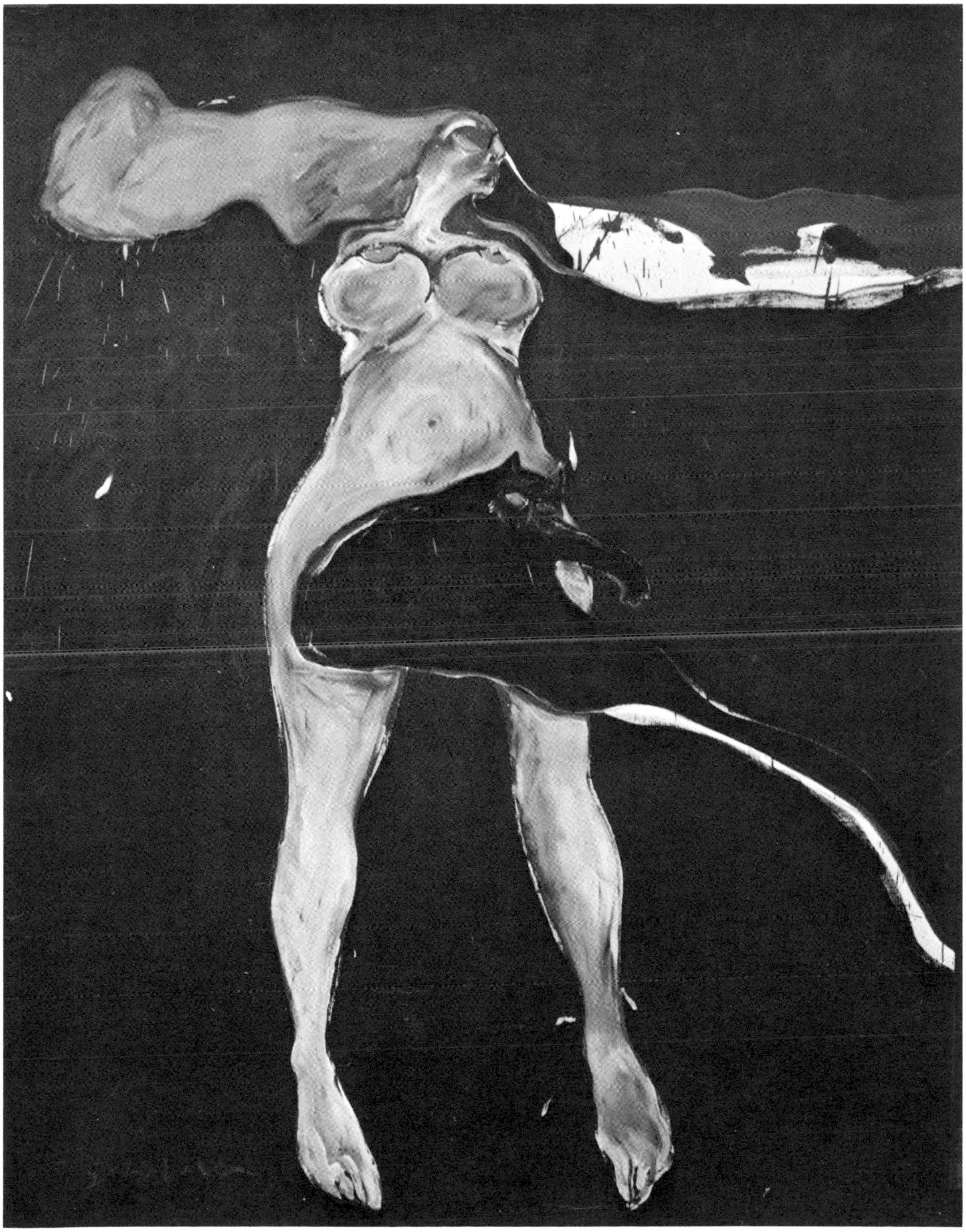

FRITZ SCHOLDER

LITHOGRAPHS

Suite of eight entitled "Indians Forever" (edition of 75), 1970–1971

16 BUFFALO DANCER
30 x 22   (76.2 x 55.9)
Illustrated on facing page

17 INDIAN AT THE BAR
30 x 22   (76.2 x 55.9)

18 INDIAN AT THE CIRCUS
30 x 22   (76.2 x 55.9)

19 INDIAN WITH FEATHER
30 x 22   (76.2 x 55.9)

20 INDIAN WITH PIGEON
22 x 30   (55.9 x 76.2)

21 INDIANS WITH UMBRELLAS
22 x 30   (55.9 x 76.2)

22 KACHINA DANCERS
22 x 30   (55.9 x 76.2)

23 WAITING INDIAN
30 x 22   (76.2 x 55.9)

Other lithographs, 1971

24 INDIAN AND WOMAN
30 x 22   (76.2 x 55.9)

25 SCREAMING ARTIST
30 x 22   (76.2 x 55.9)

26 SELF-PORTRAIT
30 x 22   (76.2 x 55.9) [on silver foil]

27 WILD INDIAN
30 x 22   (76.2 x 55.9)

All lithographs lent by the artist.

T. C. CANNON

PAINTINGS

28 INDIAN MAN 1966
Oil on canvas
40 x 40 (101.6 x 101.6)
Lent by Institute of American Indian Arts,
Santa Fe, New Mexico

29 MAMA AND PAPA HAVE THE GOING
HOME TO SHIPROCK BLUES 1966
Oil on canvas
84 x 59½ (103.2 x 151.1)
Lent by Institute of American Indian Arts,
Santa Fe, New Mexico
Illustrated on page 33

30 ANDREW MYRICK
(Let Them Eat Grass!) 1970
Acrylic on canvas
46 x 40½ (116.8 x 103.9)
Lent by the artist
Illustrated on page 34

31 CROSS THE POWDER . . . . AND IT IS
WAR! 1970
Liquitex on canvas
38 x 38 (96.5 x 96.5)
Lent by the United States Department of the
Interior, Indian Arts and Crafts Board,
Southern Plains Indian Museum and Crafts
Center, Anadarko, Oklahoma

32 SOLDIERS 1970
Oil on canvas
48 x 36 (121.9 x 91.4)
Lent by the artist
Illustrated on page 35

33 THREE GHOST FIGURES 1970
Oil on canvas
61 x 48 (155.0 x 121.9)
Lent by the artist
Illustrated on page 36

34 WAITING INDIANS IN HOSPITAL
1970
Mixed media on canvas
40 x 36 (101.6 x 91.4)
Lent by the artist
Illustrated on page 37

35 LAW NORTH OF THE ROSEBUD
1971
Acrylic on canvas
46 x 40 (116.8 x 101.6)
Lent by the artist

36 MAN, I'D LIKE TO HAVE THAT
PINTO PONY 1971
Oil on canvas
44 x 42 (111.7 x 106.7)
Lent by the artist

37 MINE EYES HAVE SEEN THE GLORY
1971
Oil on canvas
42¾ x 44¼ (108.6 x 112.4)
Lent by the United States Department of
the Interior, Indian Arts and Crafts Board,
Southern Plains Indian Museum and Crafts
Center, Anadarko, Oklahoma

38 SIOUX 1971
Acrylic on canvas
48 x 44   (121.1 x 111.8)
Lent by the artist

39 WICHITA GHOST DANCER 1971
Oil on canvas
36 x 36   (91.4 x 91.4)
Lent by the artist

40 ALL THE TIRED HORSES IN THE SUN
1971–1972
Oil on canvas
44 x 42   (111.7 x 106.7)
Lent by the artist

41 MINNESOTA SIOUX 1971–1972
Oil on canvas
44 x 42   (111.7 x 106.7)
Lent by the artist

_____

A small group of T. C. Cannon's prints is also included in the exhibition.

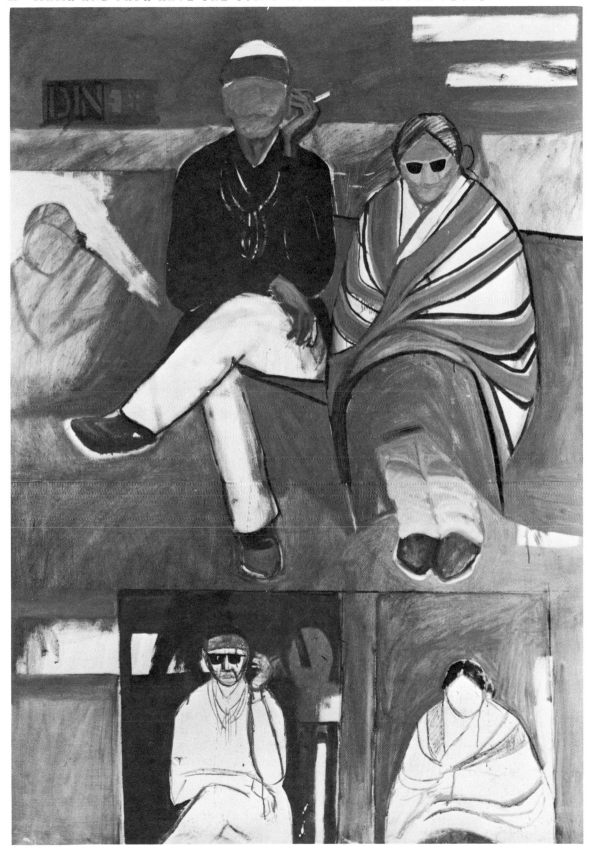

SELECTED BIBLIOGRAPHY

BOOKS

Brody, J.J. *Indian Painters & White Patrons.* Albuquerque: University of New Mexico Press, 1971 (Scholder illustration, *Screaming Indian*).

Geis, Audrey J. and Cleatus R. Richards. *Indian Justice: A Guide to Planning.* Santa Fe: National Indian Justice Planning Association Incorporated, 1971. (Illustrations and layout by Fritz Scholder.)

Gridley, Marion E. *Indians of Today.* Chicago: Indian Council Fire Press, 4th edition, 1971.

Klein, Bernard, and Daniel Icolari, editors. *Encyclopedia of the American Indian.* New York: B. Klein and Company, 1967.

Scholder, Fritz. "Native Arts in America," *Indian Voices: The First Convocation of American Indian Scholars.* San Francisco: The Indian Historical Press, 1970.

PERIODICALS

Motive (Chicago), February 1961, p. 9 (Scholder illustration, untitled drawing).

"Artists in the art news," *Art News* (New York City), vol. 61, no. 5 (September 1962), p. 9.

P[olley], E.M. "Fritz Scholder, Willis Nelson, Alden Mikkelson, Barrios Gallery, Sacramento," *Artforum* (San Francisco), vol. 1, no. 12 (June 1963), p. 54.

Moore, Irene. "The Ladies Launch a Gallery," *American Forests* (Washington, D.C.), March 1965, pp. 22–25 (Scholder illustration, *Snow Path*).

"People and Places," *New Mexico Magazine* (Santa Fe), October 1965, p. 30.

"Scholder and Bushman Exhibit at the University of New Mexico," *Southwestern Art* (Austin), vol. 1, no. 2 (Summer 1966), pp. 101–102 (Scholder illustration, one painting of New Mexico series).

"Institute of American Indian Arts Sends Exhibit to International Events," *Smoke Signals* (Newark), Fall–Winter 1966, p. 36.

"Artists West of the Mississippi Exhibition at Colorado Springs," *Southwestern Art* (Austin), vol. 2, no. 1 (November 1967), p. 84.

Snodgrass, Jeanne O. "American Indian Painters: A Biographical Directory," *Contributions* (Museum of the American Indian, Heye Foundation, New York), vol. 21, pt. 1, 1968.

"A Portfolio of IAIA Students and Their Work," *Native American Arts I* (Indian Arts and Crafts Board, United States Department of the Interior), 1968, p. 26 (Cannon illustration, *Trail of Tears*).

"News and Notes," *Southwestern Art* (Austin), vol. 2, no. 2 (March 1968), p. 69 (Scholder illustration, *Indian #16,* cat. no. 2).

"Grand Prize Winner, 1967 Biennial Exhibition of American Indian Art, Washington, D.C.," *Smoke Signals* (Newark), Spring 1968, p. 42 (Scholder illustration, *Indian #16,* cat. no. 2).

Wenzell, C.R. *Artists of Santa Fe* (Santa Fe), 1969, p. 42.

Ewing, Robert A. "The New Indian Art," *El Palacio* (Museum of New Mexico, Santa Fe), vol. 76, no. 1 (Spring 1969), pp. 33–38 (Scholder illustration, *Moccasin Pattern; Insane Indian; Indian and Rhinoceros,* cat. no. 4; and *The Faculty of the Institute of American Indian Arts at 4:15 P.M.*).

Coates, Robert M. "Indian Affairs, New Style," *The New Yorker* (New York City), June 17, 1969, pp. 102–112.

Stewart, Kenneth M. "Scalps and Scalpers, in the Mohave Indian Culture," *El Palacio* (Museum of New Mexico, Santa Fe), Summer 1969, pp. 25–30 (Scholder illustration, three drawings).

Boulay, Peter C. "Indians Forever, Part one, Problems, Problems," *Arizona Teacher* (Phoenix), October–November, 1969, pp. 14–17 (Scholder illustration, *Indians Forever*).

"Fritz Scholder—New Indian Oils," *Southwestern Art* (Austin), vol. 2 (1970), no. 4, pp. 56–57 (Scholder illustration, *New Mexico #42, Indian with a Dog,* and *Kiva at San Ildefonso Pueblo*).

Constable, Rosalind. "Forum: The Vanishing Indian," *Art in America* (New York City), vol. 58, no. 1 (January–February 1970), p. 45.

N[emser], C[indy]. "Fritz Scholder at Nordness," *Arts Magazine* (New York City), vol. 44, no. 5 (March 1970), p. 61.

Meigs, John. "Experience in Excellence: An Artist's View," *New Mexico Magazine* (Santa Fe), May–June 1970, p. 25 (Scholder illustration, *Super Pueblo #2*).

Waugh, Lynne and John. "Renaissance of the Indian Spirit," *American Education* (United States Department of Health, Education, and Welfare, Office of Education, Washington, D.C.), July 1970, pp. 15–20.

Nordness, Lee. "Lee Nordness," *Arts Magazine* (New York City), vol. 45, no. 6 (April 1971), p. 71.

Motive (Chicago), April–May 1971 (Scholder illustration, *American Indian,* cat. no. 9, *Waiting Indian #4*).

Waugh, Lynne. "Will Success Spoil Fritz Scholder," *New Mexico Magazine* (Santa Fe), vol. 49, no. 5-6 (May–June 1971), pp. 36–40 (Scholder illustration, *Kiva at San Ildefonso and Dog; Black-*

feet Tepee; Indian Called Horse After McCormick [construction]; *Indian in Gallup,* cat. no. 10; *Indian on Horseback;* and *American Indian,* cat. no. 9).

New, Lloyd. "A New Vitality Rekindles Proud Fires of the Past," *House Beautiful* (Chicago), June 1971, pp. 134–135 (Scholder illustration, *Indian with Strawberry Soda Pop;* and *American Indian,* cat. no. 9).

Price, Vincent. "The Lure and Lore of Indian Art," *The American Way* (American Airlines, New York City), vol. 4, no. 6 (June 1971), p. 14.

Scholder, Fritz. "Indian Art: Self-Interview, and Emergence of the New Indian Painting," *South Dakota Review* [issue: "American Indian II"] (University of South Dakota, Vermillion), vol. 9, no. 2 (Summer 1971), pp. 75–86 (Scholder illustration, paintings: *Screaming Indian No. 1; Indian #19,* cat. no. 3; *Buffalo Dancer;* and *Screaming Indian No. 2;* lithographs from "Indians Forever": *Waiting Indian,* cat. no. 23; *Kachina Dancers,* cat. no. 22; *Indian at the Circus,* cat. no. 18; *Indian Riders with Umbrellas* [sic], cat. no. 21; *Indian at the Bar,* cat. no. 17; *Indian and Pigeon* [sic], cat. no. 20; and *Buffalo Dancer,* cat. no. 16).

Jamison, Margaret, and R. Eric Gustafson. "Santa Fe: The Southwest and Its Re-Interpretation in Art," *Southwest Art Gallery Magazine* (Houston), September 1971, pp. 18–19 (Scholder illustration, *Indian at Taos Pueblo*).

Kieve, Rudolf. "A Very Personal Collection," *Southwest Art Gallery Magazine* (Houston), September 1971, pp. 20–22.

Roberts, Bob. "Taos Revisited," *Southwest Art Gallery Magazine* (Houston), September 1971.

Waugh, Lynne. "Arts Unlimited," *Southwest Art Gallery Magazine* (Houston), September 1971, p. 18.

"Tamarind: America's Voice of Lithography," *Southwest Art Gallery Magazine* (Houston), October 1971, pp. 14–17 (Scholder illustration, *Indian at the Bar,* cat. no. 17).

EXHIBITIONS

Sacramento City College [Scholder one-man exhibition], 1958.

Artists' Cooperative Gallery, Sacramento [Scholder one-man exhibition], 1959.

E.B. Crocker Art Gallery, Sacramento [Scholder one-man exhibition], 1959.

Philbrook Art Center, Tulsa, "14th Annual National Competition—American Indian Painting and Sculpture," May 5–31, 1959.

Garden and Arts Center, Sacramento [Scholder one-man exhibition], 1960.

Tucson Art Center, Inc., "10th Annual Southwestern Painters' Show," April 10–May 1, 1960.

Roswell Museum and Art Center, "1st Annual Southwestern States Exhibition," October 14–November 23, 1962.

Museum of Fine Arts of Houston, "The Southwest: Painting and Sculpture," December 7, 1962–January 20, 1963 [Scholder: Ford Foundation Purchase Award].

Hali's 261 Gallery, Tucson [Scholder one-man exhibition], 1963.

Dallas Museum of Fine Arts, "13th Southwestern Exhibition of Prints and Drawings," January 17–February 17, 1963 [Scholder: Edwin B. Hopkins Purchase Award in Drawing].

Huntington Galleries, "Centennial Exhibition of Painting and Sculpture," January 24–February 24, 1963 [Scholder: First prize for painting by an American artist].

University of Arizona, Tucson [Scholder one-man exhibition], 1964.

Dulin Gallery of Art, Knoxville, "1st National Watercolor Exhibition," September 20–October 15, 6–December 16, 1966.

William Rockhill Nelson Gallery of Art, Kansas City, "15th Mid-America Annual Exhibition," May 14–June 13, 1965 [Scholder: Hallmark Purchase Award].

Museum of New Mexico, Santa Fe, "1965 New Mexico Fiesta—Biennial Exhibition," June 25–September 12, 1965.

Art Gallery, United States Department of the Interior, Washington, D.C., "2nd Annual Invitational Exhibition of American Indian Painting," November 30, 1965–January 28, 1966.

Scottsdale [Arizona], "5th Annual Scottsdale National Indian Arts Exhibition," 1966 [Scholder: First prize in experimental work].

Museum of New Mexico, Santa Fe, "Young Indian Painters," February 13–March 27, 1966.

Weatherspoon Art Gallery, University of North Carolina, Greensboro, "Art on Paper," November 1964.

Kaloa Building, Anchorage, "Indian and Eskimo Arts and Crafts Exhibition from the Bureau of Indian Affairs," June 8–August 31, 1967. [Exhibition toured in Europe and South America.]

Colorado Springs Fine Arts Center, "Twenty-first/Artists West of the Mississippi," July 6–September 6, 1967.

Liberal Arts Center, College of Santa Fe, "An exhibition of Paintings—Fritz Scholder," September 17–30, 1967.

Center for Arts of Indian America, United States Department of the Interior, Washington, D.C., "1967 Biennial Exhibition of American Indian Arts and Crafts," November 6–December 15, 1967 [Scholder: Grand Award].

Scottsdale [Arizona], "7th Annual Scottsdale National Indian Arts Exhibition," April–March 10, 1968 [Scholder: Special award in polymer painting].

Center for Arts of Indian America, United States Department of the Interior, Washington, D.C., "Fritz Scholder, James McGrath, Otellie Loloma—Three From Santa Fe," May 6–June 28, 1968.

Philbrook Art Center, Tulsa, "23rd Annual American Indian Artists Exhibition," May 7–June 9, 1968 [Juror's statement by Fritz Scholder].

Anderson Gallery, Roswell Museum and Art Center, "Fritz Scholder," December 8, 1968–January 9, 1969.

Scottsdale [Arizona], "8th Annual Scottsdale National Indian Arts Exhibition," 1969.

El Paso Museum of Art, "14th Annual Sun Carnival Art Exhibition," December 7, 1969–January 4, 1970 [Scholder: Prize].

Esther Bear Gallery, Santa Barbara [Scholder one-man exhibition], 1970.

The Marion Koogler McNay Art Institute, San Antonio, "Masterpieces from the Museum of New Mexico," February 8–March 8, 1970.

Lee Nordness Galleries, New York City, "Fritz Scholder—New Indian Oils," February 28–March 19, 1970.

Museum of New Mexico, Santa Fe, "1970 Southwest Fine Arts Biennial," May 17–September 1970 [Scholder: Juror's Award].

Janus Gallery, Santa Fe [Scholder one-man exhibition], opened August 16, 1970.

Art Gallery, New Mexico Highlands University, Las Vegas [Scholder one-man exhibition], November 1–December 4, 1970.

Larkins Gallery, Santa Fe, "American Before Columbus," November 1–22, 1970.

Esther Bear Gallery, Santa Barbara, "Fritz Scholder—Paintings," January 24–February 15, 1971.

The Store, Santa Barbara, "Fritz Scholder—Paintings," January 24–February 15, 1971.

Indian Art Gallery, Heard Museum, Phoenix [Fritz Scholder one-man exhibition], March 6–31, 1971.

Museum of the American Indian, Heye Foundation, New York City [Group exhibition], May 1–June 30, 1971.

Museum of New Mexico, Santa Fe, "Fine Arts Biennial," May 23–September 13, 1971 [Scholder: Juror's Award].

The Jamison Galleries, Santa Fe, "Indians & Women—Paintings & Drawings by Fritz Scholder," June 19–July 3, 1971.

Gallery of Contemporary Art, Taos, "Fritz Scholder: Exhibition of New Paintings, Drawings & Lithographs," September–December 19, 1971.

E.B. Crocker Art Gallery, Sacramento, "Collectors," September 18–October 17, 1971.

Oklahoma Art Center, Oklahoma City, "13th Annual Eight State Exhibition of Painting and Sculpture," September 24–October 31, 1971.

Library Gallery, Southwest Missouri State College, Springfield [Scholder one-man exhibition], October–November 18, 1971.

Philbrook Art Center, Tulsa, "Texas Collects," October 2–26, 1971.

Union Galleries, University of Texas at El Paso, "A Blending of Cultures—A Blending of Time," October 24–November 5, 1971.

The Jamison Galleries, Santa Fe, "Scholder at Tamarind," November 27–December 11, 1971.

Fendrick Gallery, Washington, D.C., "Indians Forever: Patricia Benson and Fritz Scholder," September 7–25, 1971.

Southern Plains Indian Museum Arts and Crafts Center, Anadarko, "Paintings and Graphics by T.C. Cannon," November 18–December 18, 1971.

INDEX OF TITLES

Reference is to catalog number. T.C. Cannon's prints not included.
Black-and-white illustration indicated by asterisk (*); color illustration by double asterisk (**).